New Mexican Food Made Easy

SECOND EDITION

Introduction

This book does what it says, makes New Mexican Food Easy! It's written in a way that will allow the beginner to choose how much of each recipe to make with fresh ingredients, or simply replace with store-bought ones. You can also mix and match recipes in this book to create your own unique masterpieces. The ingredients listed in the recipes should be available throughout the US in most major grocery stores.

New Mexico has a wealth of history and culture to share, created by the intermingling of Native, Hispanic and Ranching populations. This heritage has created foods as unique and colorful as the breathtaking landscapes that grace the state. This cookbook is an introduction to the amazing food that New Mexicans enjoy every day, so you can carry on creating the delicious traditional tastes of the Southwest wherever you may be.

New Mexican Food Made Easy was born from the constant bragging I have done over the last umpteen years about New Mexico and its amazing foods. I was often frying up Sopapillas or drinking Horchata with roommates when I was in college out of state. Even on trips abroad I just had to share a bit of New Mexican culture and food with the locals so they could have a little taste of where I came from.

My hope is that you'll take this book home with you wherever that is, and be able to share a little piece of the Land of Enchantment with your friends and family just as I have done and that you can rejoice together in friendship and great food.

Pick

Roast

Green Chile

Steam

Peel

Pick Your Chiles

Chiles are an essential part of the New Mexican way of life. There are hundreds of varieties (or cultivars) that have been perfected over the centuries by local farmers in small river valleys. Hatch chiles, named after the valley in which they are grown, are famous for their superior flavor and are shipped worldwide. Large green varieties such as Sandia, Big Jim, or Anaheim are very popular come autumn harvest time for bulk roasting, but any variety of red or green chiles can be roasted. On the next page, you will find a helpful chile reference chart for this book. Chiles can range from mild to hot, so be sure to check the label or ask the grocer before making your selection. For chile lovers, bulk chile roasting is an annual cultural event and is best done as a family or with a group; prepping all that chile is quite a lot of work for one person!

Chile Roasting

While you can roast a few chiles anytime you need them, most people wait for peak chile harvest season (July through September), when local grocery stores stock bushels of chile for bulk processing. Chiles are roasted to remove their tough outer skins, enhance their flavor, and soften the inner flesh. They can be roasted anywhere, as long as you have an open flame or strong heat source. Roast a few at a time over a backyard grill, on a wire rack set over a stovetop burner, with an oven broiler, or even on a comal (a flat round cast iron griddle used for cooking tamales). Turn the chiles often to ensure even roasting. If you want to roast in bulk, a barrel roaster will get the job done fast. Barrel roasting is usually offered as a free service if you purchase chiles in bulk.

Roasting 101

Steam'em Good

Chiles have very tough skins that need to be roasted until charred black to separate the skin from the soft flesh underneath. After they are charred they will be hot; quickly and carefully place them in an enclosed container to trap the steam. The steam further helps the skins to loosen, making peeling easier. Keep them covered until the chiles are cool enough to handle, about 10 minutes for a small batch. Bulk batches are placed in large food-safe plastic bags and tied close. The chiles steam and cool as you drive home from the market and should be ready for the next step when you arrive home.

Peel and Freeze

Set a large colander into your sink to catch the peels and stems, and a large clean bowl and cutting board on the counter. Put on a pair of gloves and peel the chiles by rubbing them with your fingers under a gentle stream of water over the colander, removing the stems as well. Removing the seeds is optional; if you like more heat, leave them in the chiles. Place the peeled chiles into the bowl on the counter. Then chop them on the cutting board, if desired, or leave them whole. Cook chiles immediately into a recipe or stuff them into freezer bags, removing as much excess air as possible. Once frozen chiles are thawed, they need to be used within a day or two and shouldn't be re-frozen.

Chile Reference Chart

Only the varieties referenced in this book are shown here.

MILD

Poblano

Ancho (dried Poblano)

MILD TO **HOT**

Hatch

New Mexico or Ristra

MEDIUM TO **HOT**

Jalapeño

Serrano

Contents

To ensure you have a solid foundation for cooking world-renowned New Mexican food, I have created a free online companion course for this book which includes step-by-step video tutorials, lists of helpful resources and bonus recipes so you can present beautiful, flavorful, and amazing food on your table to enjoy with friends and family.

This free course will be invaluable in your first steps toward success and to build confidence in the kitchen. I want you to have fun learning how to cook delicious New Mexican food! I highly recommend you take advantage and sign up for the course which is available right now.

Visit the following link to gain access to this free New Mexican Food Made Easy Companion Course and begin your journey now.

www.GoldilocksKitchen.com/free

Foreword

Nothing connects us more than being able to break bread with friends and family, old and new. When we sit together and share a meal, we connect with the food and, if we are lucky, the culture represented by those dishes. This is a book that allows you to do just that. Emily Sego has spent much of her life in New Mexico and generously shares her deep knowledge and passion for the food and culture of the Land of Enchantment. I travel a lot and always love to collect cookbooks from those trips, but I have just returned from Georgia O'Keeffe's Abiquiu and Ghost Ranch empty-handed. I'm thrilled there is now a book that fills that gap.

New Mexican Food Made Easy is the perfect book to paint a colorful picture of the food of the desert. With more than 50 recipes, beautifully photographed and clearly detailed, this book provides the building blocks of learning to cook like a New Mexican local. Starting with a primer on chiles, the journey continues with breads (tortillas, sopapillas and a fry bread), sauces, salsas and sides so you can learn to layer the flavors and textures into dishes of your own. Not feeling creative? This book guides you through enchiladas, ribs, tostadas and rellenos, along with many more combos, using the bright, colorful, and textured ingredients indigenous to the Southwest.

How exciting that we can journey with Emily through New Mexico with a front-row seat on this guided tour of the New Mexican pantry!! If you can't make it to New Mexico, why not let it come to you, and gather your tribe around a vibrant, inspired table, loaded with the fragrant and enchanted dishes found in this book? You will not be sorry!!

Katy Keck

Chef Katy Keck, Author and Global Flavor Expert

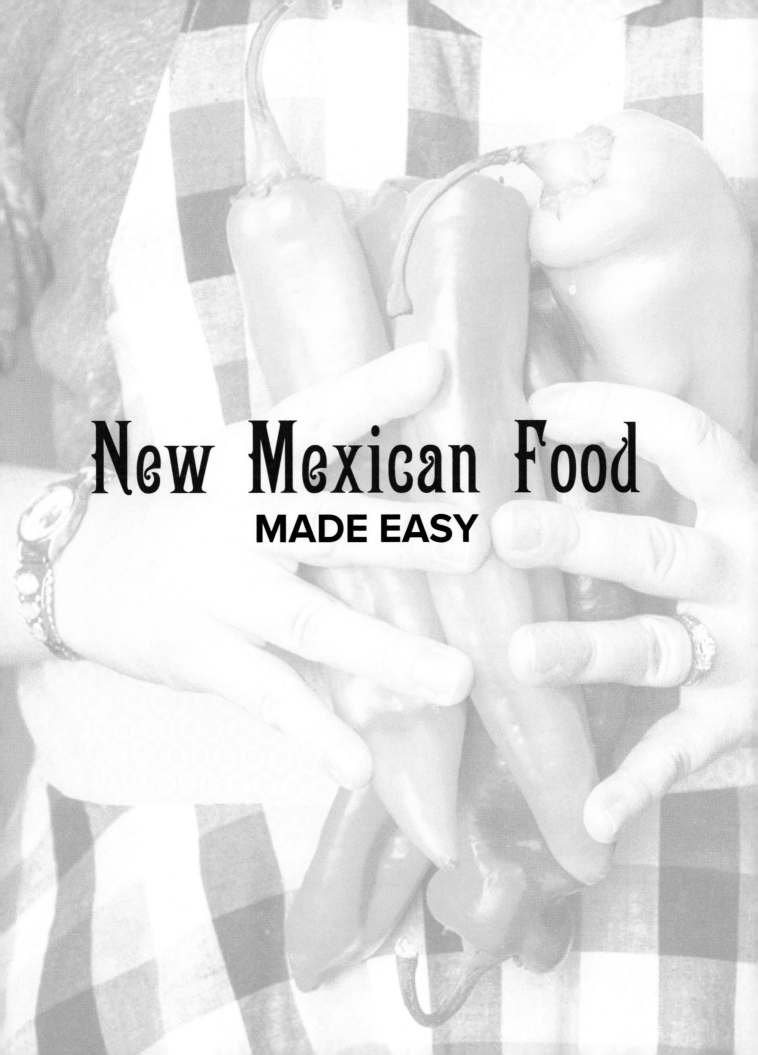

New Mexican Food
MADE EASY

Breads

Blue Corn (Atole) Cornbread

1 ¼ cups blue cornmeal

1 cup all-purpose flour

3 teaspoons baking powder

½ teaspoon baking soda

1 teaspoon salt

1 ¼ cups milk

2 large eggs

3 tablespoons honey

7 tablespoons unsalted butter, melted

1 cup shredded Cheddar Jack cheese

4 jalapeños, cored, seeded and chopped

Prep time: 10 minutes   Cook time: 35 minutes   Serves: 9

I love to bake this cornbread right in my 9-inch cast-iron skillet, melting the stick of butter in it and pouring the melted butter into the cornbread batter. If you do this, be sure to leave 1 tablespoon in the skillet to swirl around to "grease" it. If you don't have a 9-inch cast-iron skillet, bake it in an 8X8-inch square baking pan (like a brownie pan) or an 8-inch round cake pan and increase the bake time by about 5 minutes.

1. Set your oven to 350°F. In a medium mixing bowl, whisk together the blue cornmeal, flour, baking powder, baking soda and salt. If you have a sifter, run the mixture through two or three times, discarding the coarse grains left at the bottom each time.

2. Whisk together the milk, eggs, and honey. Grease your skillet or pan with a tablespoon of melted butter. Pour the rest of the butter into the milk-egg-honey mixture and whisk to combine.

3. Whisk the dry flour mixture into the wet milk mixture. Stir in the cheese and jalapeños. Empty the batter into your greased pan or skillet and bake for about 30-35 minutes, or until the edges have pulled away and are slightly brown. Remove and let it cool at least 10 minutes before cutting and serving.

New Mexican Sopapillas

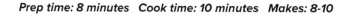

4 cups sifted flour

1 tablespoon baking powder

1 teaspoon salt

1 tablespoon sugar

2 tablespoons vegetable oil

1 $\frac{1}{3}$ cups warm water

Vegetable oil or shortening (at least 2 $\frac{1}{2}$ cups)

Prep time: 8 minutes   Cook time: 10 minutes   Makes: 8-10

Sopapillas are sections of thin simple dough that fill up with air like a balloon when placed in hot oil, leaving a large cavity inside. Bite off a corner and drizzle the inside with honey, or stuff with savory food and smother with chile sauce for a fantastic meal.

1. In a medium mixing bowl whisk the flour, baking powder, salt, and sugar together. Create a small depression in the center and pour in the 2 tablespoons of vegetable oil. Whisk in the oil. It will incorporate unevenly into little clumps; this is okay.

2. Gently pour in the warm water and knead the dough until it is smooth. Divide the dough in half, and seal each half in a zipper-lock bag to rest the dough while you heat the oil for frying.

3. Fill a Dutch oven or deep-sided frying pan with oil at least 2 inches deep. Set over medium-high heat. If you have a food thermometer, heat the oil to about 375°F.* Remove one portion of dough and roll out on a clean, flourless surface. Roll the dough to a thickness of $\frac{1}{8}$ inch. Using a pizza cutter, cut the dough into squares approximately 4X4 inches.

4. Place a sheet of plastic wrap over the rolled out dough. Gently slide an individual square of dough into the hot oil. It should rise to the top and begin to puff up almost immediately. Use a large spoon or tongs to carefully splash oil over the top; this really helps the sopapillas puff.

5. Once it's finished puffing up, flip and fry until both sides are light golden brown. Place in a large bowl lined with paper towels. Repeat with the remaining dough. Serve immediately with honey.

*Note: If you don't have a food thermometer, there's a simple way to test the oil to see if it's at the proper temperature for frying. Place the handle of a wooden spoon into the oil. When it fizzes immediately, it's ready.

Bisquick Sopapillas

2 cups Bisquick mix

1/2 cup warm water

1 tablespoon sugar

Vegetable oil or shortening (at least 2 1/2 cups)

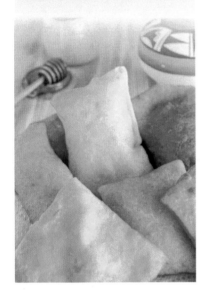

Prep time: 15 minutes Cook time: 5 minutes Makes: 8 sopapillas

Bisquick sopapillas are a cinch to whip up if you are in a hurry. They fry faster than authentic New Mexican Sopapillas; you'll be flipping them over to brown the other side just as soon as they puff. These sopapillas are a little fluffier on the inside than their original counterparts.

1. In a medium mixing bowl, stir together Bisquick and warm water until it forms a dough ball.

2. Sprinkle about a tablespoon of Bisquick onto a clean flat surface and knead the dough by hand for a few seconds until dough is moist but no longer sticky. Divide in half and place each into a zippered baggie to let the dough rest for about 5-10 minutes.

3. Fill a Dutch oven or deep-sided frying pan with oil at least 2 inches deep. Set to medium-high heat. If you have a food thermometer, heat the oil to 375°F. Remove one portion of dough and roll out on a clean, flourless surface. Roll the dough to a thickness of 1/8 inch. Using a pizza cutter, cut the dough into squares approximately 4X4 inches.

4. Place a sheet of plastic wrap over the rolled out dough to keep it from drying out. Gently slide an individual square of dough into the hot oil. Use a large spoon or tongs to carefully splash oil over the top, to help the sopapillas puff. Immediately flip over and brown the other side. Remove the sopapilla and place in a paper towel lined bowl to cool. Repeat with remaining dough. Serve immediately with honey.

Homemade Corn Tortillas

2 cups masa harina

1 $^2/_3$ cups warm water

1 teaspoon lime juice

$^1/_2$ teaspoon salt

1 gallon-sized plastic zippered bag

Masa harina is a finely ground corn "flour" that is found in the Mexican aisle or section of your local grocery store. There's no need for a tortilla press to produce perfect rounds, just a pot lid with a sharp edge to use as a tortilla cutter. Your first few may be fails, but practice makes perfect!

1. Set a cast-iron skillet or large griddle to medium-high heat. Mix all ingredients together in a bowl with a large spoon. The dough should come together in a smooth mass. If it's crumbly, work in more water a tablespoon at a time. It should have a consistency similar to chocolate chip cookie dough.

2. Divide the dough in half, then half again to create four equal sized chunks. Place chunks in a zippered bag. Remove one chunk and divide it into three uniform chunks and roll each into a ball. Cover with plastic wrap while you roll out the tortillas.

3. Cut a gallon sized zippered baggie apart along three edges so it will open like a book. Open and place a ball of dough in the center of one side. Fold the plastic over so the dough is between two pieces of plastic. Gently press dough ball with your hand to flatten, then roll with a rolling pin, turning the plastic a little with each roll until you get a roughly 5- to 6-inch tortilla. If you have a small pot lid with a sharp edge, you can place this over the raw tortilla and cut into a round shape. Run your finger around the outside of the lid to remove excess dough.

4. Place a hand underneath the plastic and tortilla. Place your other hand over the open tortilla. Flip it over and slowly peel off the back portion of plastic. With a rolling motion, place the tortilla onto the hot skillet or griddle. Toast on each side for about 30 seconds. Tortilla may puff and hiss; this is normal. Set on a cooling rack to cool and store, or cook into a recipe.

*Note: If tortilla rips, the dough is either too dry, too wet, or too thin. This dough can dry out very quickly. Working a splash of water in as needed can revive it, and since there's no gluten, it can be worked for as long as you like and will never get tough.

Indian Fry Bread

2 cups white flour, Bluebird brand if possible

$\frac{1}{2}$ teaspoon salt

2 tablespoons powdered milk mix

2 teaspoons baking powder

1 cup water

Vegetable oil for frying

Prep time: 12 minutes   Cook time: 5 minutes   Serves: 6

One of the best things about New Mexico is being able to stop along the side of a rural highway and purchase fresh Fry Bread. Now you can re-create this iconic bread at home whenever you get a hankerin' for it.

1. Prepare a large deep skillet or Dutch oven for frying by filling with oil at least 1 inch deep and setting it over medium heat. While the oil heats, continue with the recipe.

2. Sift the flour, salt, powdered milk, and baking powder together in a large bowl. Pour in the water and mix with a fork until the dough just comes together. With a heavily floured hand, roll the dough around the bowl until it forms one large ball, being careful not to knead it at all or very little. It should be a very wet dough covered with flour on the outside to keep it from sticking to your hands or the bowl.

3. Place the dough ball on a floured work surface and cut the dough into six equal parts. Flour your hands. Working with one piece at a time, work the dough into a thin circular shape a little smaller than a dinner plate. Pull the dough apart in the middle to create a small hole about $\frac{1}{4}$-inch in size. When the oil has reached a temperature of about 350°F, carefully slip the dough into the hot oil. The oil should start to boil immediately, or the oil is not heated enough.

4. Press the fry bread down into the oil with a metal spatula. Fry until puffy and golden. Remove to a paper towel lined plate. Serve warm with honey and powdered sugar, or load it up with classic taco fixings for a "Navajo Taco."

Easy Fresh Flour Tortillas

2 3/4 cups flour

1 1/2 teaspoons salt

6 tablespoons vegetable shortening, cut into 6 pieces

3/4 cup plus 2 tablespoons warm water

1 teaspoon vegetable oil

Prep time: 45 minutes Cook time: 20 minutes Makes: 6-8 tortillas

These homemade tortillas will be an easy, fresh, and delicious addition to any New Mexican meal.

1. Whisk flour and salt in a large mixing bowl. Add the pieces of shortening and using a fork mix the shortening into the flour mixture until it resembles coarse meal. Stir in the water with a mixing spoon until combined into a ball of dough.

2. Empty dough out onto a clean flourless surface and briefly hand knead until it's a smooth ball. Pull off chunks of dough 2 to 3 tablespoons in size and roll into balls. Place dough balls on a plate; cover and refrigerate at least 30 minutes. They can also be stored overnight.

3. On a lightly floured surface, thinly roll out a ball of dough (should be about 8 inches across). Spread oil over cooking surface of skillet with a wad of paper towels. Lay the raw tortilla in the skillet and cook until it begins to bubble, about one minute. Flip and cook on the other side until puffy and browned in spots, about another minute. Transfer to a plate and cover with foil to keep warm. Repeat with the remaining dough balls.

*Note: The cooked flour tortillas can be layered between parchment paper, covered with plastic wrap, and kept in the fridge for a few days. Just re-heat in the microwave and serve.

Fillings

Green Chile Beef Picadillo

1/3 cup shelled piñon (pine) nuts

2 tablespoons vegetable oil

1/2 onion, minced

1 pound ground beef

2 cloves garlic, minced or pressed

1 teaspoon cinnamon

1/2 teaspoon cumin

1/4 teaspoon ground coriander

1/2 teaspoon salt

1 cup diced canned tomatoes

1 tablespoon vinegar

1 tablespoon brown sugar

1/2 cup roasted chopped green chiles

1/3 cup raisins

Picadillo is a savory meat stuffing made with spices, nuts or potatoes. This New Mexican version includes green chile and piñon (pine) nuts. It has many applications, such as stuffing into sopapillas or empanadas. Picadillo also makes a great stuffing for Chile Rellenos for Two (page 72); for this variation I'd recommend replacing the green chile with some shredded Monterey Jack cheese, letting it melt into the meat mixture before stuffing into the chiles.

1. Heat a large skillet over medium-high heat. Place the piñon nuts in the skillet for about 5 minutes, stirring frequently. Remove the nuts and add the vegetable oil and onion. Cook until the onion is soft and translucent, about 3-5 minutes.

2. Add the ground beef and cook until no pink remains. Stir in the garlic, cinnamon, cumin, coriander, and salt. Cook for 30 seconds. Stir in the tomatoes, vinegar, brown sugar, and green chiles. Cover and cook over low heat, stirring often, for 10 minutes.

3. Uncover and turn off the heat. Stir in the raisins and piñon nuts. Serve filling plain with tortillas or use as a stuffing into your desired recipe.

Carne Adovada

1 (5 to 6 pound) boneless pork butt roast

3 tablespoons kosher salt

4 cups water

4 ounces dried New Mexico red chile pods

2 teaspoons dried oregano

6 cloves garlic

2 tablespoons honey

2 tablespoons vinegar

2 teaspoons cumin

Pinch of ground cloves

1 teaspoon table salt

1 teaspoon chicken bouillon powder

2 limes

It's hard to think of anything more delicious than tender pork meat that has been marinated and cooked in red chile sauce. Feeling bold? If so, you can take this recipe to the next level by shredding the finished meat and placing it onto a parchment lined baking sheet (in a single layer), and broiling it in your oven for a few minutes until the top of the meat is well browned. You'll then have delicious "Carnitas!"

1. Cut the meat into 1-inch cubes and toss with the kosher salt in a large mixing bowl. Cover and leave on the counter while you proceed with steps two and three.

2. Fill a medium saucepan with 4 cups of water and the bouillon powder; set it over medium-high heat. While the water heats, break the stems off the chiles and dump the seeds out. Rip the chile pods into pieces, and place the pieces into the boiling water. Turn the heat off and cover the saucepan with a lid. Soak covered, for 30 minutes. Pour 1 $\frac{1}{2}$ cups of the soaking broth out through a strainer and set aside. Strain the rest of the water out and discard it.

3. Set your oven to heat to 325°F. Place the soaked chile pods, 1 cup of the saved soaking water, oregano, whole garlic cloves, honey, vinegar, cumin, cloves, and table salt in a blender. Blend for 1 to 2 minutes, or until a thick uniform paste forms. Then blend in the additional $\frac{1}{2}$ cup of the soaking water.

4. Stir together the pork cubes and contents of the blender in an oven-safe baking dish or pot. Bake uncovered for 2½ hours. Remove from oven to cool. Serve with freshly sliced lime wedges.

Calabacitas con Frijoles

1 medium butternut squash, peeled and cut into $1/2$-inch cubes

2 tablespoons vegetable oil, divided

Salt and pepper

$1/4$ cup uncooked instant or long-grain white rice

$1 1/4$ cups vegetable broth

$1/2$ yellow onion, minced

2 garlic cloves, minced or pressed

2 teaspoons ground cumin

1 tablespoon chile powder, or to taste

1 tablespoon chopped fresh oregano

1 (15 ounce) can black beans, drained and rinsed

$3/4$ cup crumbled queso fresco cheese

1 tablespoon chopped cilantro

Prep time: 20 minutes   Cook time: 45 minutes   Serves: 8

This vegetarian sopapilla stuffing consists of beans, rice and roasted butternut squash seasoned with the native flavors of New Mexico. It works great as a side dish for Red Chile Ribs (page 67) or stir in some Green Chile Sauce (page 33) and use it as a filling for a veggie burrito.

1. Heat oven to 425°F. In a medium mixing bowl, toss cubed squash with 1 tablespoon vegetable oil and season with salt and pepper. Roast in a single layer on a rimmed baking sheet for 45 minutes.

2. While the squash is roasting, cook rice on the stovetop according to package directions, using vegetable broth instead of water.

3. In a frying pan set over medium heat, add 1 tablespoon vegetable oil and onion. Sprinkle with a pinch of salt and cook until soft and translucent. Add the garlic, cumin, chile powder, and oregano. Cook for 30 seconds or until fragrant. Stir in the beans and cooked rice. Crumble the cheese over the top. Turn the heat to low until the squash is done roasting.

4. In a large bowl, combine squash with bean and rice mixture. Sprinkle with chopped cilantro. Serve.

Creamy Southwestern Chicken

1 ½ pounds boneless skinless chicken breast

Salt and pepper

¼ cup frozen or canned corn

¼ cup canned black beans, drained and rinsed

¾ cup of your favorite salsa

¼ cup sour cream

Prep time: 5 minutes   Cook time: 6-8 hours   Serves: 8

Great on its own or stuffed into a sopapilla (page 16), this recipe is my family's personal favorite - you can't go wrong with chicken slow cooked in salsa, then smothered in chile sauce. This recipe is great for a weekday dinner too. Just put the chicken in the slow cooker before you leave for work and then prepare the sopapillas when you get home.

1. Season chicken with salt and pepper and place it in a slow cooker. Mix the corn, beans, and salsa together and pour over the top of the chicken. Cook on low for 6 to 8 hours.

2. Just before serving, fry up the sopapillas and set aside. With a fork in each hand, shred the chicken into small pieces, or empty the contents of the slow cooker into a stand mixer fitted with the paddle attachment to shred the chicken. Mix in the sour cream.

3. If stuffing into sopapillas, cut through the center of a sopapilla and stuff each side with the Creamy Southwestern Chicken. Serve side by side, smothered with your choice of chile sauce.

Sauces & Creams

Classic Green Chile Sauce

2 tablespoons vegetable oil

¹/₄ cup minced onion

2 cloves garlic, pressed or minced

¹/₄ teaspoon ground cumin

¹/₄ teaspoon dried oregano

1 ¹/₂ cups (12 ounces) roasted, peeled and chopped green chile, fresh or canned

1 tablespoons flour

¹/₂ cup chicken broth

¹/₄ teaspoon salt

¹/₄ teaspoon pepper

Prep time: 5 minutes   Cook time: 30 minutes   Makes: 2 cups

Green chiles are actually red chiles picked when not quite ripe. Their pungent flavor is enhanced with roasting, and when cooked into this savory sauce you can smother the amazing flavor all over your food; it's delicious with just about anything.

1. Heat oil in a skillet over medium-high heat. When the oil is hot, add the onion and a pinch of salt. Cook for about 5 minutes to soften and brown the onion.

2. Add the garlic, cumin, and oregano and stir for about 30 seconds to bloom the flavors.

3. Stir in the green chile, then sprinkle the flour over the top and stir for about 2 minutes. The food will clump up; this is normal.

4. Slowly pour in the chicken broth, whisking constantly. When combined, season with salt and pepper. Bring to a boil, cover, and simmer over low heat for about 20 minutes. Serve immediately or store frozen up to 3 months.

Green Enchilada Sauce

1-2 fresh tomatillos or 1 (7 ounce) can of tomatillos

2 tablespoons vegetable oil

$^1/_4$ cup minced onion

2 cloves garlic, pressed or minced

$^1/_4$ teaspoon ground cumin

$^1/_4$ teaspoon dried oregano

1 cup (8 ounces) roasted, peeled and chopped green chile

2 tablespoons flour

1 cup chicken broth

$^1/_2$ teaspoon salt

$^1/_4$ teaspoon pepper

Prep time: 5 minutes   Cook time: 30 minutes   Makes: about 2 cups

Tomatillos are not green tomatoes, although they look similar and are in the same botanical family. This recipe pairs well with Chicken Enchiladas (page 59).

1. If using fresh tomatillos, remove the outer husk and blanch tomatillos by placing them in boiling water for 5 minutes to soften them. Remove and puree in a blender. If using canned, skip blanching and add contents to blender and puree.

2. Heat oil in a skillet over medium-high heat. When the oil is hot, add the onion and a pinch of salt. Cook for about 5 to 6 minutes to soften the onion.

3. Add the garlic, cumin, and oregano and stir for about 30 seconds to bloom the flavors.

4. Stir in the green chile, then sprinkle the flour over the top and whisk for about 1-2 minutes. The food will clump up; this is normal.

5. Slowly pour in the chicken broth and the tomatillo puree, whisking constantly. When combined, season with $^1/_2$ teaspoon salt and $^1/_4$ teaspoon pepper. Bring to a boil, cover, and simmer over low heat for about 20 minutes. Serve or store in freezer bags up to three months.

Green Chile Cream Sauce

1 tablespoon unsalted butter

1/2 yellow onion, minced

1/2 cup chopped, roasted green chile

1/2 cup chicken broth or stock

1 cup heavy cream

1 garlic clove peeled, left whole

1 lime, zested and juiced

Salt

Prep time: 8 minutes   Cook time: 10 minutes   Makes: 2 1/2 cups

Green Chile Sauce is as important to New Mexicans as wine is to the French. This sauce has a little bit of both cultures, blending a traditional New Mexican staple with a little European flair. This sauce is best served immediately.

1. In a large frying pan, add butter and set heat to medium-high. Cook onion and sprinkle with salt, stirring often, until soft and beginning to brown.

2. Add green chile and chicken broth. Bring to a boil and reduce heat to simmer. Cook until about 2 tablespoons of liquid remain.

3. Add the cream and whole garlic clove and return to a boil. Reduce liquid to about half and remove from heat.

4. Carefully pour sauce into a blender and add the lime zest and juice. Process until smooth. Season with salt as desired. Serve hot.

Red Chile Sauce (from pods)

3 cups water

2 teaspoons dried Mexican oregano

$^1/_2$ cup chopped onion

4 garlic cloves, chopped

2 teaspoons cumin

$^1/_2$ teaspoon ground coriander

$^1/_2$ teaspoon salt

1 teaspoon chicken bouillon powder

4 ounces dried New Mexico red chile pods or Ancho chile pods

1 tablespoon honey

Prep time: 15 minutes   Cook time: 20 minutes   Makes: 3 cups

The chile ristras you see hanging all over porches are more than just decoration. Dried chile pods were traditionally pulled off of ristras as needed to cook up a fresh batch of Red Chile Sauce. Here I have streamlined the traditional recipe, which uses whole chile pods with fresh authentic ingredients, and made it a bit simpler without sacrificing any flavor. If you can't find Mexican oregano, simply substitute regular dried oregano. The difference in taste will be minimal.

1. In a medium saucepan, add 3 cups of water, oregano, onion, garlic, cumin, coriander, salt and bouillon powder. Bring to a boil.

2. While the water mixture is heating, rip dried chile pods apart into 1-inch pieces and remove the stems and seeds (you may want to wear gloves). When water mixture comes to a boil, stir in chile pieces and cover. Turn heat to low and simmer for 10 minutes.

3. Remove the chile-broth mixture from heat and carefully pour broth through a fine-mesh strainer into a 4-cup measuring cup or mixing bowl.

4. Place all solids into a blender. Add 1 cup of strained broth into the blender along with the honey. Blend for about one minute, or until sauce is pureed and very thick. Blend in 1 additional cup of strained broth and taste. Add more salt to taste or more broth if desired for a looser consistency and discard the remaining broth. Sauce can be stored in an airtight container in the fridge for up to 3 days.

Red Chile Sauce (from powder)

3 tablespoons vegetable oil

$^1/_2$ cup minced onion

Pinch or two of salt

3 cloves garlic, minced or pressed

1 teaspoon dried oregano

$^1/_2$ teaspoon ground cumin

$^1/_2$ cup ground red chile powder

$^1/_4$ teaspoon chipotle chile powder

2 tablespoons flour

2 cups water or chicken broth

1 tablespoon honey or agave nectar

Many find making red chile sauce with chile (or chili) powder is more convenient than making it from dried chile pods since ground chile powder can be found anywhere all year long. If you can get your hands on some ground Chimayo red chile powder you'll be following traditional Northern NM cooks who highly prize its regional flavor (which is definitely on the hot side). However, the addition of flour to thicken the sauce also adds a slightly bitter taste, which necessitates adding a little extra honey or agave nectar to bring balance and a bonus of additional flavor to your sauce.

1. Heat vegetable oil in a large skillet on medium heat and stir in onion. Sprinkle with a pinch or two of salt and cook, stirring occasionally, until translucent and browned on the edges, about 10 minutes.

2. Add the garlic, oregano, and cumin. Cook, stirring often, for about 1 minute.

3. With a whisk, stir in the red chile powder, chipotle chile powder, flour and broth, stirring mixture until no lumps remain. Whisk in the honey and bring sauce to a boil. Reduce heat to low and simmer for about 20-30 minutes to slightly thicken the sauce. Remove from heat and season with salt and additional honey, if desired, to taste.

Red Enchilada Sauce

1 1/2 cups water

1 teaspoon dried Mexican oregano

2 garlic cloves, chopped

1 teaspoon cumin

Pinch of ground coriander

1 teaspoon salt

1 teaspoon beef or chicken bouillon powder

2 ounces dried New Mexico red chile pods

1 (15 ounce) can of tomato sauce

1 tablespoon honey

1 tablespoon red wine or apple cider vinegar

Prep time: 15 minutes Cook time: 10 minutes Makes: 2 1/2 cups

Some traditional cooks simply use red chile sauce to make their enchiladas. Many popular store-bought enchilada sauces add additional ingredients like tomato and vinegar to red chile sauce, so I created a homemade version of store-bought sauce that will give you full-bodied, deeply flavored, amazing enchiladas.

1. In a medium saucepan add 1 1/2 cups of water, oregano, garlic, cumin, coriander, salt, and bouillon powder. Bring to a boil.

2. Rip dried chile pods apart into 1-inch pieces and remove the stems and seeds (you may want to wear gloves). When water mixture comes to a boil, stir in chile and cover. Turn heat to low and simmer for 10 minutes.

3. Pour water mixture through a fine-mesh strainer into a 2 cup measuring cup or mixing bowl; set broth aside. Place all solids into a blender. Add 1/2 cup of strained broth into the blender. Blend for about 1 minute, or until sauce is pureed and very thick. Add the tomato sauce, honey, vinegar, and the rest of the strained broth. Sauce can be stored in an airtight container in the fridge for up to 3 days.

Chipotle Cream Sauce

1 cup Mexican Crema
(page 44), or sour cream at
room temperature

$1/2$ cup mayonnaise

3 whole canned chipotle
chiles in adobo sauce

$1/4$ teaspoon salt

$1/8$ teaspoon black pepper

Prep time: 5 minutes   Cook time: 10 minutes   Makes: 1 $3/4$ cups

A delicious homemade creamy sauce with a kick, it can be substituted for a sour cream garnish or used in enchiladas or any stuffing recipe where more chile heat is desired. Chipotle chiles are ripe, red jalapeño peppers preserved in adobo sauce. They are sold in most grocery stores in the Mexican aisle in small cans.

1. Combine all ingredients in a food processor (or a good blender will do in a pinch) and blend until smooth.

2. Pour out into a medium sized saucepan and set to medium-low heat to warm, stirring often. Remove from heat; do not boil. Serve as a garnish.

Fruit Salsa

1 cup chopped pineapple

1 mango, rind and pit removed

1 peach, peeled and halved

$1/2$ red bell pepper, cored and seeded

$1/4$ red onion

1 serrano, cored and seeded, stem removed

$1/4$ cup cilantro leaves

Juice of one lime

Pinch of salt

Prep time: 10 minutes   Makes: about 2 cups

This salsa recipe is an amazing blend of sweet and hot. Excellent with tortilla chips; it also makes a tasty garnish for Tostadas (page 64), or Red Chile Ribs (page 67).

Place all ingredients into a food processor and process until desired consistency. Serve fresh, or chill for 1 hour to help flavors mingle even further. Will keep stored in the refrigerator for 3 days.

*Note: All ingredients can be chopped and mixed by hand if using a food processor isn't an option.

Fresh Garden Salsa

1 clove garlic

1 fresh green chile, seeded and cored

2 green onions, chopped

1 jalapeño, cored and seeds removed

2 large ripe tomatoes, cored and seeds removed

1 (4 ounce) can diced green chiles

1 teaspoon olive oil

Juice from 1 lime

$\frac{1}{4}$ cup fresh cilantro leaves

Salt and pepper to taste

Prep time: 10 minutes   Makes: about 2 cups

Fresh salsa is always best eaten within a day of its creation. This versatile salsa is great with chips or as a garnish for just about anything.

1. Place garlic, green chile, green onions, and jalapeño in the bowl of a food processor and pulse a few times to coarsely chop ingredients.

2. Add the tomatoes, green chiles, olive oil, lime juice, cilantro, and a pinch of salt and pepper. Process until all ingredients are finely chopped.

*Note: All ingredients can be chopped and mixed by hand if using a food processor isn't an option.

Black Bean & Corn Salsa

1/2 red onion

1 red bell pepper

1-2 jalapeños

4 cups diced fresh tomato or 2 (16 ounce) cans diced tomatoes

1-2 cloves fresh garlic (about a tablespoon)

2 tablespoons extra virgin olive oil

Juice from two limes

2 teaspoons ground cumin

1 can sweet corn, drained

1 can black beans, drained and rinsed

1 teaspoon salt, or to taste

Prep time: 10 minutes   Makes: about 4 cups

My personal favorite salsa, hearty black beans and sweet corn bring a wonderful earthy and sweet flavor to the fresh peppers and seasonings in this salsa.

1. Combine the onion, bell pepper, jalapeño, tomatoes, garlic, olive oil, lime juice, and cumin in a food processor and process until roughly chopped.*

2. Pour into a large bowl. Stir in the corn and black beans. Season to taste with salt. Serve fresh.

*Note: All ingredients can be chopped and mixed by hand if using a food processor isn't an option.

Mexican Crema

1 cup pasteurized heavy cream

2 tablespoons buttermilk

$1/8$ teaspoon salt

Juice from one fresh lime

Prep time: 24 hours   Makes: about 1 1/4 cup

Mexican Crema is a Mexican cultured cream similar to sour cream. It is sold commercially in just about any grocery store, but it's fun to be able to make it fresh at home. It's the perfect garnish for just about every New Mexican entreé.

Stir together the cream and buttermilk. Cover and leave out on the counter to thicken about 1 day (24 hours). Juice one lime and mix the salt into the juice. Stir the juice into the cream. Serve or refrigerate for up to 2 months.

Taco Crema

1/3 cup Mexican Crema
(page 44) or sour cream

1/3 cup mayonnaise

1 tablespoon taco seasoning

Juice from one fresh lime

Prep time: 5 minutes   *Makes: 2/3 cup*

A cool yet spicy addition drizzled onto any type of tacos, or really anything with a Mexican flair. This crema topping can be whipped up in no time.

In a small bowl, whisk all ingredients together until smooth. Drizzle over tacos as desired.

Bacon Green Chile Guacamole

4 slices bacon, chopped

3 small ripe avocados

$1/4$ cup chopped roasted green chile

3 tablespoons chopped fresh cilantro

2 tablespoons minced red onion

2 tablespoons lime juice

3 garlic cloves, minced or pressed

Pinch of salt

1 teaspoon ground cumin

1 small tomato, cored and cut into $1/4$-inch pieces

Prep time: 20 minutes   Serves: 6

The cool creamy flavors of traditional guacamole are amazing on their own, but when you add bacon and green chile, this recipe really puts it over the top. After mixing in the final diced avocado, season to taste with additional salt, lime juice or cumin if desired.

1. In a large skillet set to medium heat, brown chopped bacon until crispy. Remove to cool on a paper towel-lined plate.

2. Mash the flesh from 1 avocado with the green chile, cilantro, onion, lime juice, garlic, salt, and cumin in a medium mixing bowl.

3. Peel and pit the other two avocados and dice into $1/2$-inch cubes. Gently stir in the diced avocado, tomato, and chopped bacon with the mashed avocado mixture from step 2. If not serving immediately, press plastic wrap onto the entire surface and refrigerate for up to 24 hours.

Roasted Tomatillo Salsa

4 fresh tomatillos

$^1/_2$ serrano chile (ribs, seeds and stem removed)

$^1/_2$ onion

1 garlic clove

Small handful of fresh cilantro

$^1/_2$ avocado

Juice from $^1/_2$ lime

Salt to taste

Prep time: 5 minutes   Cook time: 15 minutes   Makes: 6 servings

The humble tomatillo looks like a green tomato with a thin, papery brown husk emanating from the stem end. They are very bitter when fresh, but make a fun and unique salsa when roasted and used in this recipe.

1. Preheat oven to 400°F. Pull the husks off the tomatillos. Wash the skins and remove the cores.

2. Place the tomatillos on a rimmed baking sheet and roast for 15 minutes.

3. Place roasted tomatillos in a food processor with one half the serrano chile, onion, garlic, cilantro, avocado, lime juice, and a pinch of salt. Blend and taste a sample. Add more salt or heat with the other half of the serrano chile as desired. Serve fresh.

Breakfast

Huevos Rancheros

2 tablespoons butter

2 medium russet potatoes, peeled and diced to $1/_8$-inch

$1/_2$ bell pepper cored, seeded and diced

1 jalapeño, cored, seeded and diced (optional)

$1/_2$ medium onion, minced

$1/_4$ cup vegetable oil

Salt and pepper

6 corn tortillas

6 eggs, cracked into a bowl

$1 1/_2$ cups Homestyle Refried Beans (page 74), or 1 (15 ounce) can

1 cup Green Chile Sauce (page 33) or Red Chile sauce (page 36)

Huevos Rancheros (or ranch eggs) is one of my very favorite breakfast recipes. Fried eggs are served on corn tortillas spread with refried beans and often served with a side of fried potato hash. It's then smothered in hot chile sauce to give you a good wake-up call in the morning.

1. Adjust an oven rack to the middle position and preheat oven to 450°F.

2. Heat a large 12-inch non-stick skillet over medium-high heat and add the butter. When the butter is just melted, add the potatoes, bell pepper, jalapeño, and onion. Season lightly with salt and stir occasionally until the potatoes become crisp and golden brown.

3. While the potato mixture cooks, brush or spray vegetable oil on both sides of the tortillas and sprinkle with a pinch of salt. Place them on a flat baking sheet and bake the tortillas for about 2 minutes, flipping them over halfway through. Remove from the baking sheet and cover to keep warm.

4. When the potatoes are browned and crispy, make six little open spaces for the eggs to be cooked and pour them in quickly, one egg at a time. Sprinkle each with salt and freshly ground pepper. Turn the heat down to low and cover the skillet. Cook the eggs for about 1 to 2 minutes for runny yolks, 4 minutes for hard yolks.

5. While the eggs cook, spread each tortilla with warmed refried beans. Remove eggs and hash with a spatula and serve on individual tortillas. Top with green chile sauce or salsa and serve.

Ham and Egg Breakfast Burrito

2 tablespoons vegetable oil

1 medium russet potato, peeled and diced

8 eggs

3 tablespoons half & half

$^1/_2$ cup diced ham

1 tablespoon unsalted butter

$^1/_3$ cup Green Chile Sauce (page 33)

$^1/_2$ cup Cheddar Jack cheese

4 burrito-sized flour tortillas

Salt and pepper

Prep time: 5 minutes   Cook time: 25 minutes   Serves: 4 burritos

The original breakfast on the go, the breakfast burrito of New Mexico can be made with countless combinations of fillings, all garnished with either red or green chile sauce (asking for "Christmas" will get you both).

1. Place a large non-stick skillet over medium-high heat. Heat the oil, then add the diced potato. Sprinkle with salt. Cook, stirring every two minutes, for about 6-8 minutes, or until golden brown and soft.

2. Remove potatoes and set aside. Whisk the eggs, half & half and ham together just until incorporated. Add butter to the hot skillet and let it melt. Pour in the egg mixture, season with salt and pepper, and stir constantly until cooked through. Remove from heat.

3. Following the pictures below, place heaping spoonfuls of egg mixture, potatoes, green chile sauce and cheese in the center of a tortilla. Spread outward into a loose rectangle slightly below the center.

4. Fold sides of the burrito in just over the edges of the filling, then fold the bottom up to partially cover the filling. Roll the burrito upwards tightly, folding in any corners of tortilla that stick out.

5. Serve immediately, or wrap the burrito with foil and keep warm in a 275°F oven for up to 1 hour. For a make-ahead breakfast, wrap the burrito tightly in foil and freeze. Remove foil but do not discard. Wrap the burrito with a paper towel and heat in the microwave. Wrap hot burrito with foil and take it on the go.

Chorizo Breakfast Sopapillas

3 tablespoons ground chorizo sausage

6 eggs

$\frac{1}{4}$ cup half & half

1 cup salsa

1 diced avocado

Freshly fried sopapillas (page 16)

Prep time: 25 minutes   Cook time: 10 minutes   Serves: 4

Chorizo is a sausage usually made with pork and hot red chile. It can come either loosely ground or processed into links. This stuffing is great in either a burrito or sopapilla.

1. In a medium non-stick skillet, cook chorizo sausage over medium-high heat for about 5-6 minutes.

2. While the sausage is cooking, combine eggs and half & half in a mixing bowl and gently whisk until just combined. When the sausage is cooked, pour the egg mixture into the skillet and stir until they are fully set, about 2 minutes.

3. Remove from heat and dollop salsa over the top. Sprinkle with avocado. Spoon filling into sopapillas and serve with salsa.

Piñon Blue Corn Pancakes

Prep time: 15 minutes   Cook time: 25 minutes   Serves: 16-20 pancakes

1 1/2 cups all-purpose flour

1 cup blue corn flour

1 tablespoon baking powder

1/4 tablespoon baking soda

1 teaspoon salt

2 eggs lightly beaten

2 1/4 cups milk

2 tablespoons apple cider vinegar

2 teaspoons vanilla

3 tablespoons honey

5 tablespoons unsalted butter, melted and divided

1/2 cup piñon (pine) nuts

1 cup fresh blueberries

Blue Cornmeal or flour (also called "Atole") is mixed with white flour and piñon nuts to create a uniquely hearty and delicious New Mexican pancake favored by locals around Santa Fe.

1. Set a griddle to medium heat (or alternately set a non-stick skillet over medium heat.) Sift all-purpose flour, blue corn flour, baking powder, baking soda, and salt together in a mixing bowl.

2. In a separate mixing bowl whisk together the eggs, milk, vinegar, vanilla, honey, 4 tablespoons of melted butter, and piñon nuts. Let this mixture rest on the counter at room temperature for 10 minutes.

3. Gently stir the flour mixture into the milk/egg mixture until just combined. Use the last tablespoon of melted butter to grease your hot griddle or frying pan.

4. Pour batter onto hot griddle using a 1/3 cup measuring cup. Flip over when the underside is golden brown and edges are no longer shiny. Serve stacks of fresh pancakes with warm maple syrup and garnish with blueberries.

Lunch & Dinner

New Mexican Arroz con Pollo

6-8 bone-in, skin-on chicken thighs

$1/3$ cup all-purpose flour

2 tablespoons Sazón seasoning, divided

2 tablespoons vegetable oil

$1/2$ onion, chopped

1 bell pepper, seeded, cored and chopped

1 generous pinch of saffron threads

2 garlic cloves, pressed

$1/3$ cup chopped roasted green chile (or one small 4 ounce can)

2 $1/2$ cups chicken broth

2 bay leaves

2 cups Jasmine rice, or other long grain rice (not instant)

2-3 fresh tomatoes, seeded, cored and chopped (optional)

1 cup frozen peas

Salt and pepper

Prep time: 15 minutes   Cook time: 30 minutes   Serves: 6-8

Arroz con Pollo (Chicken and Rice) is a savory dish that the Spanish settlers brought to New Mexico with them. Sazón seasoning can be found in the Mexican seasoning section at your local grocery store. If you would like to substitute boneless chicken breast meat, decrease cooking time in step 2 to 3-5 minutes per side.

1. Pat chicken dry with paper towels and season with salt and pepper. Mix 1 tablespoon of Sazón seasoning into flour. Dredge chicken in seasoned flour and set aside. Preheat oven to 350°F.

2. Add vegetable oil to a large Dutch oven set over medium-high heat. Brown chicken pieces in a single layer, for about 7 minutes, until golden brown. Flip once and brown the other sides for an additional 3-5 minutes. Remove to a plate and set aside.

3. Add chopped onion and bell pepper to the pot and sprinkle with a pinch of salt. Cook, stirring often, until soft and onion begins to brown. Add saffron threads by crushing them in your palm first, then add the garlic and green chile. Cook until fragrant, about 30 seconds, then add in the chicken broth, scraping all the browned bits off the bottom of the pan. Stir in the bay leaves, rice, tomatoes and remaining Sazón. Nestle chicken and juices back into the pot.

4. Bring to a boil, then cover and place in the oven for 20 minutes. Transfer chicken to a plate. Stir frozen peas into the rice. Cover and let them heat through for about 3 minutes. Season rice to taste with salt and pepper and serve with chicken.

Classic Red Chile Enchiladas

Prep time: 25 minutes   Cook time: 15 minutes   Serves: 6-8

12 corn tortillas

Vegetable oil for frying

2 ¹/₂ cups Red Enchilada Sauce (page 38) or 2 (15 ounce) cans

1 pound shredded Monterey Jack cheese

1 small yellow onion, minced

Shredded lettuce, sour cream, cilantro, sliced black olives for garnish

A fantastic vegetarian dish, the simple flavors of chile sauce, corn tortillas, and cheese really shine. For a truly authentic recipe, use blue corn tortillas.

1. Preheat oven to 350°F. In a small skillet set over medium-high heat, add vegetable oil to reach a depth of 1/4 inch. In an additional medium skillet set over medium-low heat, pour in 1 cup of enchilada sauce to warm.

2. Set out a clean casserole dish next to the stove. Organize an assembly line with the heated oil, then warm enchilada sauce, the casserole dish, and a bowl of cheese-onion filling, in that order.

3. When the oil is heated (oil will bubble quickly when tortillas are added), quickly dip a corn tortilla in on both sides with tongs and remove, letting the excess oil drip back into the pan. Then dip both sides of the fried tortilla into the warm red enchilada sauce and lay the tortilla in the casserole dish. Place a small amount of shredded cheese and onion down the center and roll the tortilla. Continue frying, dipping, and stuffing tortillas until you have filled the dish with a single layer, closely nesting the rolled tortillas.

4. Pour the rest of the sauce over both ends of the tortillas in the dish. Generously sprinkle Monterey Jack cheese down the center and bake in the oven for 15 minutes. Enchiladas are done when heated through and cheese is melty on top. Garnish with shredded lettuce, sour cream, cilantro, and sliced olives if desired.

Green Chile Chicken Enchiladas

Prep time: 25 minutes   Cook time: 5 minutes   Serves: 4

12 6-inch corn tortillas

1 tablespoon vegetable oil + at least $\frac{1}{4}$ cup for shallow frying

1 pound boneless skinless chicken breast with rib meat*

1 tablespoon Weber Kick'n Chicken seasoning

2 $\frac{1}{2}$ cups Green Enchilada Sauce (page 34), or about two 15 ounce cans)

$\frac{1}{2}$ cup crumbled queso fresco

1 cup sour cream + more for garnish

1 $\frac{1}{2}$ cups shredded Monterey Jack cheese

Chopped lettuce, black olives, sour cream and cilantro or parsley to garnish

These enchiladas are prepared using the regional rolled technique of central and southern New Mexico and are a little messy to make, yet exceptionally delicious. This recipe will quickly become a family favorite.

1. Preheat oven to 350°F. In a medium skillet, heat 1 tablespoon oil over medium-high heat. Generously season both sides of the chicken with chicken seasoning. Place in hot skillet and leave it alone for 5-7 minutes. Check underneath; when chicken is golden brown flip and cook the other side for an additional 5 minutes or until internal temp has reached 165°F. Remove chicken to cool.

2. Pour in 1 cup of green enchilada sauce. Scrape the bottom of the pan and mix into the sauce. Set the sauce over low heat. Shred the chicken.

3. In another medium-size skillet over medium-high heat, add vegetable oil to reach a depth of $\frac{1}{4}$ inch. Set out a separate clean oven safe plate next to the stove for building the enchiladas.

4. When the oil is heated, quickly dip a corn tortilla in on both sides with tongs and remove, letting the excess oil drip back into the pan. Then dip both sides of the tortilla into the warm green enchilada sauce and lay on the plate next to the stove.

5. Place a small amount of shredded chicken, queso fresco, and sour cream down the center and fold in half. Repeat two more times so you have three enchiladas on the plate. Sprinkle with cheese and add any desired sides, such as Refritos (page 74) or New Mexican Rice (page 77).

6. Place in the oven to melt the cheese and heat the sides, 3-5 minutes. Repeat with remaining enchiladas until tortillas are used up. Serve with garnishes.

*Note: If raw chicken breast is more than 1 inch thick on one end, the thick end should be pounded thin between two pieces of plastic wrap to create a uniform thickness across the breast and ensure even cooking.

Chicken Enchilada Casserole

1 1/3 cups chicken broth

1 cup roasted, chopped green chiles

1 tablespoon onion powder

1 teaspoon garlic powder

1 cup fat-free sour cream

1/2 teaspoon ground cumin

2 cans cream of chicken soup

1 rotisserie chicken, meat shredded and removed from bones

3/4 teaspoon salt

1/2 teaspoon freshly ground black pepper

Vegetable oil for frying

12 corn tortillas

2 cups finely shredded Cheddar Jack cheese

*Prep time: **40 minutes**   Cook Time: **30 minutes**   Serves: **10-12***

These enchiladas were a favorite college recipe for me. It's fairly simple to make, and goes even faster when you can recruit someone to pull and shred the meat from the rotisserie chicken while you mix up the filling.

1. Preheat oven to 350°F and spray a 13X9-inch baking dish with non-stick spray. In a large mixing bowl, stir together the chicken broth, green chiles, onion powder, garlic powder, sour cream, cumin, cream of chicken soup, shredded chicken, salt, and pepper, and set aside.

2. In a medium skillet, add vegetable oil to a depth of 1/4 inch. Set to medium-high heat.

3. Spread 1/2 cup chicken-soup mixture in the bottom of the prepared 13X9-inch baking dish. Fry corn tortillas one at a time in hot oil on each side for just 5-10 seconds to soften. Let excess oil drip off and place them in a single layer over soup mixture in the baking dish to cover the bottom.

4. Spread the first layer of tortillas with half of the remaining chicken-soup mixture, followed by 1 cup of cheese. Repeat layers, starting with more fried tortillas, then chicken-soup mixture, and ending with the cheese. Bake at 350°F for 25 minutes or until bubbly.

Chile Rellenos Casserole

6 eggs, yolks and whites separated

$1/2$ cup flour

$1/4$ cup milk

1 pound shredded Monterey Jack cheese

4 ounces crumbled goat cheese (or crumbled queso fresco)

$1 1/2$ cups Red Enchilada Sauce (page 38)

8-10 whole canned green chiles

Prep time: 30 minutes   Cook time: 20 minutes   Serves: 8

Chile Rellenos (whole chiles stuffed with cheese, batter dipped and fried) are traditionally time consuming and a bit tedious. This casserole has the same great taste and is easy to throw together to feed a large family.

1. Set your oven to 400˚F. Spray a 9X13-inch casserole dish with cooking spray and set aside.

2. Combine the egg yolks, flour, and milk, either by whisking or with a food processor until smooth. Leave at room temperature for 20 minutes while you proceed with the rest of the recipe.

3. In a large mixing bowl, gently toss the cheeses together. Spread 1 cup of enchilada sauce into the bottom of the casserole dish. Open the chiles by gently tearing down one side and lay 4 or 5 of them flat in a single layer over the top of the enchilada sauce. Place handfuls of cheese over the chiles, leaving about $1/2$ cup of cheese mixture for topping the casserole later. Place an additional layer of flattened green chiles over the cheese.

4. Whip the egg whites on high to stiff peaks, about 4 minutes. Stir the egg yolk mixture lightly, then gently fold into the egg whites until no white streaks remain. Spread egg batter in an even layer over the top of the chiles. Place in the oven for 15-20 minutes, or until the batter is cooked through and golden brown on top.

5. Remove the casserole from the oven. Sprinkle the remainder of the cheese mixture on top and place the casserole under the broiler for just a couple of minutes to melt and slightly brown the cheese. Let cool 5 minutes and serve with extra enchilada sauce drizzled over the top.

Green Chile Chicken Stew

Prep time: 20 minutes   Cook time: 45 minutes   Serves: 10-12

There are many versions of this hearty stew; my version cuts the average cook time from over two hours to just 40 minutes by using store-bought rotisserie chicken, which adds even more great flavor.

2 tablespoons vegetable oil

1 onion, chopped

14 ounces (about two cups) of fire roasted chopped green chiles

3 celery stalks, chopped

3 medium size carrots, peeled and chopped

2 garlic cloves, minced or pressed

1 tablespoon dried oregano

1 teaspoon cumin

1 teaspoon thyme

$1/3$ cup flour

7 cups chicken broth or stock

1 (15 ounce) can of fire roasted diced tomatoes

4 medium potatoes, peeled and diced

1 rotisserie chicken, meat shredded, bones and skin discarded

Salt and pepper

1. In a large stock pot or Dutch oven, heat 1 tablespoon vegetable oil over medium-high heat. Cook onion with a pinch of salt for about 4-5 minutes until soft. Add in green chiles, celery, carrots, and the other tablespoon of vegetable oil. Cook, stirring frequently, until onions are browning and celery and carrots are beginning to soften.

2. Add the garlic, oregano, cumin, and thyme and cook until fragrant, about 30-60 seconds. Sprinkle in the flour and cook for about 1 minute. Add the broth, the tomatoes, and potatoes, scraping up any browned bits of food stuck to the bottom of the stock pot or Dutch oven.

3. Bring the soup to a boil. Cover and cook on low for about 25 minutes, or until potatoes and carrots are soft. Season to taste with salt and pepper. Stir in the shredded chicken, cover, and cook for 5 additional minutes. Serve with warm flour tortillas.

Pork and Beans Tostadas

¼ cup vegetable oil

4 corn tortillas

1 cup Refried Beans (page 74)

1 ½ cups store-bought pork carnitas or pulled pork

1 cup shredded Monterey Jack cheese

1 cup shredded lettuce

1 cup Green Chile Cream Sauce (page 35)

½ cup chopped fresh tomato

Sour cream, chopped red onion, sliced black olives for garnish

Prep time: 10 minutes   Cook time: 10 minutes   Makes: 4 tostadas

The tostada is very similar to an open face taco, but is not usually served with ground taco meat. Instead, you can top tostadas with just about anything you can imagine. Carnitas are a great option, and are widely available pre-seasoned and packaged in grocery store meat aisles. One package is usually enough to make two New Mexican recipes.

1. Heat vegetable oil over medium-high heat until shimmering (or it reaches 375°F).

2. Fry each corn tortilla on both sides until crispy and it holds its shape. Let excess oil drip back into pan, and set on individual plates. Spread first with refried beans, then top with layers of pork carnitas, cheese, lettuce, chile sauce, tomato, and garnish with any other additional toppings as listed to the left.

Red Chile Ribs

Prep time: 24 hours   Cook time: 6 hours   Serves: 6-8

2 racks pork baby back ribs

5 tablespoons dark brown sugar

2 teaspoons dried oregano

4 teaspoons paprika

2 teaspoons mustard powder

2 teaspoons onion powder

3 teaspoons fresh ground pepper

2 teaspoons salt

2 cups red chile sauce or puree*

A well-known Albuquerque restaurant in the North Valley is famous for its Red Chile Ribs, so I set out to create a similar recipe. If you are a red chile lover, these ribs will be some of the very best you'll ever taste, and well worth the wait. I prefer to smother my ribs in homemade red chile puree, but store-bought red chile sauce works great too.

1. Heat a gas or charcoal grill to roughly 425°F. Pat ribs dry with paper towels. Remove the silver skin from the back of the ribs by slipping a sharp knife under the edge and peeling it up in chunks.

2. Combine the brown sugar, oregano, paprika, mustard powder, onion powder, salt, and pepper in a small bowl. Rub this mixture all over the ribs. Sear the ribs on the grill over direct heat for 1-2 minutes on each side, or until distinct grill marks appear.

3. Place ribs in a large roasting pan or baking dish. Smother both sides of the ribs in the red chile puree with a brush or clean fingers. Cover with plastic wrap and refrigerate for 18-24 hours.

4. Set your oven to 275°F. Remove the plastic wrap and replace with foil, crimping the edges all around the roasting pan. Place the ribs in the oven and cook for 6 hours. Remove and let them cool for about 10 minutes. Serve warm.

*Note: Red chile puree can be made by modifying the recipe for Red Chile Sauce (page 36). Follow the recipe through, skipping the onion, garlic, and seasonings and reducing the broth by $1/2$ cup before adding chiles and broth to the blender. I like to blend for just a few seconds to keep the puree a bit chunky.

30 Minute Pork Posole

Prep time: 10 minutes   Cook time: 30 minutes   Serves: 4-5

I'll never forget standing in the Albuquerque Old Town Plaza on Christmas Eve, surrounded by luminarias and holding a warm bowl of posole in my hands. This pork hominy stew is delicious and comes together quickly when using store-bought or leftover carnitas. Serve with lime wedges and flour tortillas.

1 tablespoon vegetable oil

1/4 onion, minced

2 cloves garlic, minced or pressed

1 (14 ounce) can white hominy, drained and rinsed

4 cups chicken broth

1/3 cup Red Chile Sauce (page 36)

1 tablespoon minced fresh oregano, or 1 teaspoon dried

1/2 teaspoon thyme

Salt and pepper

1 pound store-bought pork carnitas

1. Set a dutch oven or large pot over medium-high heat. Add vegetable oil, onion, and a pinch of salt. Cook until onion is soft and starting to brown. Stir in garlic and cook until fragrant for about 1 minute.

2. Stir in hominy and cook for about 5 minutes. Pour in broth, red chile sauce, oregano, thyme, and pork carnitas. Bring to a boil, then turn the heat to low and simmer for about 20 minutes. Remove from heat, season with salt and pepper to taste, and serve.

Taco Stuffed Sopapillas

1 pound ground beef

¹/₂ cup black beans, drained and rinsed

1 package taco seasoning

Mexican cheese blend

1 batch freshly fried sopapillas (page 16)

Garnish with Mexican Crema (page 44), salsa and shredded lettuce

Prep time: 5 minutes   Cook time: 20 minutes   Makes: 6-8

Taco stuffed sopapillas are amazingly delicious and are such a fun flavor combination, you'll wonder why you haven't heard of this recipe mashup before. The flavors of a Navajo taco now in a hand-held version.

1. In a skillet over medium-high heat, brown ground beef and drain fat. Add in beans and taco seasoning and cook for another 5 minutes. Sprinkle with cheese and stuff into sopapillas. Top with Mexican Crema, salsa, and shredded lettuce.

2. For a hand-held version, mix cooked taco meat with cheese, crema, beans and salsa before stuffing. The sopapilla will resemble a gordita and taste like a Navajo taco on the go.

Christmas Tamales

FILLING

1 ½ cups store-bought carnitas, cooked and shredded

⅓ cup Red Chile Sauce (page 36)

1 teaspoon freshly grated orange zest (orange peel)

2 tablespoons raisins, minced

TAMAL DOUGH

1 ½ cups Masa Harina

6 tablespoons vegetable shortening (or lard if you can find it)

½ teaspoon salt

1 teaspoon baking powder

1 cup warm broth (saved from cooking the meat if possible)

Prep time: 40 minutes   Cook time: 1 hour   Makes: 6-8 tamales

If using traditional corn husks, set them to soak in hot water before beginning the recipe. Dry, then spread masa and filling on the smooth side. Roll, then fold the bottom and tie it with a strip of corn husk if it won't stay folded on its own. If corn husks aren't available, use heavy duty aluminum foil to roll and steam tamales instead.

1. Mix all filling ingredients together and cover to keep warm.

2. Combine the Masa Harina, vegetable shortening, salt, and baking powder in the bowl of a food processor with a standard blade. Process until thoroughly mixed, about 10 seconds, then drizzle broth in while the processor is running. Dough should now be easily spreadable while still holding its shape.

3. Fill the bottom of a large stock pot with about 1 inch of water. Place a steaming rack or balls of aluminum foil on the bottom that will hold the tamales just above the surface of the water.

4. Cut out nine squares of aluminum foil measuring about 9X9 inches. Spread about 3 tablespoons of dough in the center of a foil square in a rectangle shape, leaving at least 2 inches of clean foil all around. Place about 2 tablespoons of meat filling in a line in the center, leaving at least 1 inch of uncovered tamal dough all around.

5. Fold the center of the foil over and press on the filling, sealing the meat in tamal dough. Crimp the bottom and side of foil to securely close. Set the foil-wrapped tamale upright in the stock pot ensuring it does not touch any water on the bottom. Repeat and fill the stock pot with upright tamales. Cover the pot and bring water to a boil. Turn the heat down to medium and simmer covered, for about 30 minutes. Remove hot tamales with tongs. They are done cooking when they easily unwrap without sticking. Serve warm or wrap tightly in plastic wrap to refrigerate for up to 3 days, or freeze up to 6 months.

Chile Rellenos For Two

2 whole large green chiles (Joe Parker variety works best) with strong stems

6-8 ounce freshly shredded Monterey Jack cheese

2 eggs, yolks and whites separated

$1/4$ cup flour, plus more for dredging

Pinch of salt

2 or more cups of vegetable oil for frying

$1/2$ cup Red Enchilada Sauce (page 38), or store-bought

Shredded lettuce, sour cream, chopped fresh tomato to garnish

Prep time: 45 minutes   Cook time: 10 minutes   Makes: 4 chiles

This recipe is a great introduction to the classic preparation method. Perfectly dipped and fried Chile Rellenos take practice; expect a bit of a mess and ripped chiles at first, but once mastered this recipe can easily be doubled or tripled so you can impress family and friends with your amazing relleno skills (and delicious taste).

1. Roast chiles until skins are mostly charred black. Set aside in a container topped with a lid while you continue with the recipe. (See page 4 for more information on roasting chiles.)

2. Remove charred peels from chiles and, if needed, cut a slit in one side about 2 inches long. Carefully remove the seeds inside with a spoon if you wish, or leave seeds in for more heat. Leave the stem intact and attached to the chile. Stuff each chile with cheese, being careful not to overstuff; the slit needs to be able to completely close. If the chile rips, not to worry, the batter should cover mistakes. Press the opening in the chile closed as best you can. Repeat with the other chiles.

3. Set a medium sized pot or deep-sided skillet over medium-high heat and fill with vegetable oil at least 1 $1/2$ inches deep.

4. While the oil warms, beat the egg whites until stiff peaks form. Beat in the yolks one at a time, then $1/4$ cup of flour and a pinch of salt until combined.

5. Dredge stuffed chiles in flour, being sure to evenly coat them all around and pat off the excess. Then gently dip stuffed chiles into the egg batter, covering all but the stem.

6. Place the batter-dipped chile into oil heated to about 375°F. Fry until golden brown on bottom, then flip and repeat using tongs. Remove and set the Chile Relleno over a spoonful or two of warm red chile sauce or enchilada sauce on a plate. Serve with a side of sour cream, chopped fresh tomato, salsa, etc. Repeat with the remaining chile and serve immediately.

Sides

Homestyle Refried Beans (Refritos)

4 tablespoons salted butter

¹/₂ onion, minced

2 cloves garlic, minced or pressed

¹/₂ teaspoon cumin

Pinch of cayenne

2 cans pinto or black beans (about 3 cups)

¹/₂ cup chicken broth

Salt and pepper to taste

Prep time: 5 minutes   Cook time: 7-10 minutes   Makes: 2 servings

If you're not a huge fan of refried beans, you will be after tasting just one bite of these refritos. Cooked with butter and seasoned properly, you might want to double the recipe because they're so good.

1. If using canned beans, drain and rinse the beans and set aside.

2. Add butter to a medium-sized skillet set over medium heat. Once melted, add the onion and cook, stirring often, for about 5-7 minutes, or until the onion has shrunk and is beginning to brown.

3. Add the garlic, cumin, and cayenne and cook until fragrant, about 30 seconds.

4. Add the beans and mash them with a potato masher or a large fork, mixing them with the butter and onions until a few chunks of beans remain.

5. Mix in the chicken broth and season with salt and pepper to taste.

Black Bean Sweet Potato Salad

2 sweet potatoes, peeled and cubed

$^1/_3$ red onion, sliced

3 tablespoons olive oil, divided

2 teaspoons chile powder

1 clove garlic

Juice from two fresh limes

2 tablespoons honey

1 cup black beans, rinsed and drained

1 small green bell pepper, finely chopped

1 jalapeño pepper, seeded and ribs removed

Salt and pepper

Prep time: 10 minutes   Cook time: 40 minutes   Serves: 10

Mild and strong flavors are perfectly woven together in this healthy and delicious side salad. Assemble it right before serving to keep the roasted sweet potatoes crisp.

1. Set your oven to 400°F. Toss the sweet potato and onion in a bowl with 2 tablespoons olive oil and chile powder. Place on a rimmed baking sheet in a single layer and sprinkle with a pinch of salt. Roast in the oven for about 40 minutes, stirring every 10 minutes.

2. Puree garlic, lime juice, honey, and remaining olive oil in a blender or food processor until smooth.

3. When vegetables are done roasting, remove and let cool for 5 minutes. Transfer to a large bowl and stir in the black beans, bell pepper, and jalapeño. Pour honey lime mixture over the vegetable mixture and toss to coat; season with salt and pepper. Serve immediately.

New Mexican Rice

1 cup Jasmine rice

$\frac{1}{3}$ cup salsa

1-2 tablespoons chopped green chile

2 cups chicken broth

Prep time: 10-15 minutes   Cook time: 15 minutes   Serves: 6-8

This very tasty rice is a spin on Spanish rice often served as a side dish to many main course meals in the Southwest. The addition of green chiles and chicken broth instead of water makes this rice exceptionally delicious. Any type of rice can be used, just follow the package directions for the proper cooking time.

1. Heat rice, salsa, green chile, and chicken broth in a medium saucepan and bring to a boil.

2. Cover and reduce heat to low. Cook for 15 minutes. Remove from heat and let sit for 10 minutes. Fluff with a fork and serve.

Bacon Wrapped Stuffed Jalapeños

½ cup shelled piñon (pine) nuts

½ cup cream cheese

½ cup shredded MontereyJack cheese

2 tablespoons unsalted butter

½ teaspoon ground sage

¼ teaspoon garlic powder

14 medium sized jalapeños, sliced in half through the stem end, seeds and ribs removed

14 slices of your favorite bacon

Prep time: 15 minutes Cook time: 20-25 minutes Makes: 14 jalapeños

These delicious little appetizers are great for parties or on game day. Make them as mild or hot as you like by removing (or not removing) the seeds and ribs. For a simpler version, leave out the butter, sage, garlic, and piñons in step 3.

1. Preheat oven to 350°F. Line a rimmed baking sheet with foil. Set a wire cooking rack inside and spray with non-stick spray.

2. In a skillet set to medium heat, toast the piñon nuts, stirring every few seconds, for about 5 minutes. Remove from skillet into a mixing bowl.

3. Add the cheeses to the mixing bowl with the piñon nuts, along with the butter, sage and garlic powder. Stir with a large spoon until thoroughly combined. Fill each jalapeño half with cheese and press the halves back together. Be careful not to overfill so the jalapeños will close all the way. Wrap with bacon and set on the prepared rack.

4. Bake in the oven for 35-40 minutes, or until bacon is crispy. Cool and serve.

Southwestern Chopped Salad

SALAD

6 cups spring mix lettuce

2 tablespoons shelled piñon (pine) nuts

2 ripe medium size tomatoes, diced

$1/2$ cup canned corn, drained

1 cup cubed watermelon

$1/2$ cup sliced red onion

1 avocado, cubed

VINAIGRETTE

$1/2$ cup extra virgin olive oil

$1/4$ cup cider vinegar

2 tablespoons honey

$1/2$ teaspoon salt

1 teaspoon dried oregano

1 tablespoon ground red chile

1 package seasoned tortilla strips to garnish

Prep time: 10 minutes   Makes: 4 servings

This fun and colorful salad showcases local flavors and brings them all together with a splash of chile honey vinaigrette. Seasoned tortilla strips are an essential component of this salad; I wouldn't skip them. They can usually be found in the lettuce or salad kit section at the grocery store or next to the croutons.

1. In a large mixing bowl, toss together the spring mix, piñon nuts, tomatoes, corn, watermelon, onion, and avocado.

2. Place olive oil, vinegar, honey, salt, oregano, and chile powder in a blender and blend until smooth.

3. Pour vinaigrette over salad and gently toss to combine. Sprinkle tortilla strips over top and serve.

Elotes (Mexican Street Corn)

6 quarts water

4 cobs of ripe corn

¹/₄ cup Mexican Crema
(page 44)

¹/₃ cup mayonnaise

Wooden chopsticks for
handles

2 ripe limes

¹/₄ teaspoon salt

4 tablespoons chile
powder

1 cup crumbled Cotija
cheese

2 tablespoons minced
fresh cilantro

Prep time: 15 minutes   Makes: 4 servings

Elotes are cobs of corn dressed in layers of tasty flavors and served by vendors on street corners throughout Mexico. Their quick rise to fame has spilled over into the US, and they can now be found in our favorite state as well. Even though the idea for these corn cobs didn't originate within New Mexico, I wanted to include them in this book because they continue to increase in popularity and are a fun addition to any Hispanic meal.

1. Bring 6 quarts of water to a boil in a large stock pot. Shuck the corn cobs, leaving some leaves attached at the bottom if desired. Place the corn into the boiling water and cook for about 8 minutes. Remove corn cobs and set aside to cool until they can be handled.

2. In a small bowl, mix together the Mexican Crema and mayonnaise, and slice limes into wedges. Set aside.

3. Skewer the corn cobs with chopsticks, then rub a fresh lime wedge all over the corn. Sprinkle corn with a pinch of salt. Brush or spread on a layer of mayo mixture to coat the corn cob. Sprinkle chile powder all over the mayo mixture, then sprinkle/press on a layer of cheese. Sprinkle a little cilantro over the elote to garnish and serve immediately.

Drinks

Agua de Sandia

1 large ripe watermelon

1 cup lime juice

8 cups water

1 to 2 cups sugar

Prep time: 20 minutes Makes: 8-10

It's no surprise how the Sandia Mountains east of Albuquerque got their name. They often shine a deep pink color during sunset, reminding one of watermelon. This refreshing drink translates directly to "water of watermelon," and is a fun drink to make for a summertime backyard barbecue or other large gathering. The amount of sugar added depends on how ripe or sweet your watermelon is.

1. Remove the watermelon rind and discard. Chop the fruit into chunks that will easily fit inside your blender.

2. Place 2 cups of watermelon, lime juice, and 2 cups water in a blender. Puree and pour through a fine mesh strainer into a large pitcher. Stir foamy contents of strainer to release more liquid. Repeat with the remaining watermelon and water.

3. Stir in the sugar, starting with a 1/2 cup. Add more to your taste. Serve drink immediately over ice.

Strawberry Honeydew Agua Fresca

2 ripe honeydew melons, quartered and seeded

3 cups water

3 cups hulled strawberries

$1/_2$ cup sugar

2 limes

Prep time: 10 minutes Serves: 8-10

The refreshing and sweet flavors of honeydew melon and strawberries come together in a delicious, fruity, refreshing drink.

1. In a blender, add two or three pieces of honeydew (depending on how large your blender is), 2 cups water, sugar, and juice from the limes. Puree and pour through a fine mesh strainer into a large pitcher.

2. Puree the remaining ingredients, working in batches, and pour each batch though the strainer. The agua fresca can be strained twice more back and forth from the blender to the pitcher to reduce thickness. Wash out the solids in the bottom of the strainer after each time.

3. Stir the contents of the pitcher, and let sit for five minutes. Taste, add more sugar or water as necessary. Pour over ice and serve immediately.

Fast Three-Step Horchata

2 cups uncooked Jasmine rice

2 cups sweetened vanilla almond milk

6 cups water

1 4-inch cinnamon stick

1 tablespoon vanilla extract

Zest from one lime

1 cup sugar

1 (12 ounce) can evaporated milk

Prep time: 10 minutes   Serves: 6

Horchata is a delicious rice milk drink blended with cinnamon. Its creamy taste is perfect for washing down a dish made with hot chile. Horchata usually takes hours to make, but this recipe is ready in about 10 minutes.

1. In a blender, combine the rice, almond milk, 1 cup of water, cinnamon sticks, vanilla extract and lime zest. Blend on the highest setting for about 2 minutes.

2. Pour contents through a fine mesh strainer into a large pitcher. Slowly pour the remaining 5 cups of water over the rice left in the strainer. Stir the rice in the strainer if necessary to allow the liquid to drain through. Discard the rice solids that are left.

3. Stir in the sugar and evaporated milk, stirring well to dissolve the sugar, about 30 seconds. Pour over ice and serve, refrigerating the remaining contents in the pitcher.

Mexican Hot Chocolate

Prep time: *5 minutes*   Cook time: *7-10 minutes*   Makes: *2 servings*

3 tablespoons dark cocoa powder

2 tablespoons honey

1/4 cup whole milk

1/4 teaspoon cinnamon

Pinch of ground cloves

Pinch of chile powder

2 cups half & half

1/4 teaspoon vanilla extract

Mexican Hot Chocolate is the ancestral forerunner of the modern day hot chocolate so many enjoy. Chocolate (cocoa) comes from Central America, and the Spanish settlers quickly adapted this drink from the natives and made it their own.

1. Warm all ingredients except vanilla in a medium saucepan, stirring occasionally, until steaming. Do not boil.

2. Remove from heat, stir in vanilla and serve.

Desserts

Natillas Custard

Prep time: 20 minutes   Chill time: 1 hour   Serves: 6-8

A lovely vanilla custard featured around the holidays, Natillas is yet another recipe brought from the Spanish homeland. Normally a fussy custard made from scratch, this version is much simpler and just as tasty.

CUSTARD

25-30 vanilla wafer cookies (Nilla wafers)

1 (4 ounce) box instant vanilla pudding

2 cups milk

$\frac{1}{8}$ teaspoon cinnamon + more for dusting

Pinch of nutmeg

2 tablespoons orange juice

MERINGUE

2 egg whites

$\frac{1}{4}$ cup granulated sugar

1. Line the bottom and sides of a large serving bowl or four individual serving bowls with vanilla wafers and set aside.

2. In a medium size mixing bowl, whisk together the vanilla pudding mix, milk, cinnamon and nutmeg until just combined. Whisk in the orange juice and continue to stir for one more minute, then pour into serving bowl(s), covering the vanilla wafers, and set aside.

3. Place egg whites in a bowl and whip on high with a hand held or stand mixer until they look white and jiggle when you shake the bowl (about 1-2 minutes). Gradually sprinkle in the sugar, still whipping for about 1-2 more minutes, until glossy stiff peaks form when beater is withdrawn from the bowl. (Meringue should no longer jiggle.) Place spoonfuls of meringue over the top of the custard, or load into a pastry bag and pipe on top (like frosting) for a more delicate look.

4. Place custards under a broiler for just a minute to brown the tops of the meringue if desired (watch carefully so they don't burn). Sprinkle top of dessert with cinnamon. Can serve immediately, but best when chilled for 1 hour.

Bizcochitos

1 ½ cups all-purpose flour

1 teaspoon baking powder

¼ teaspoon salt

1 stick unsalted butter (½ cup) at room temperature

⅔ cup granulated sugar

1 egg

1 teaspoon anise (aniseed)

1 teaspoon brandy or rum extract

¼ cup sugar

¼ teaspoon cinnamon

Prep time: 20 minutes   Cook time: 25 minutes   Makes: 18 cookies

Bizcochitos are a lovely cookie seen often around the holidays in New Mexico. Great on their own, they are even better when paired with a hot beverage. Aniseed is the traditional seasoning used in these cookies. Star Anise is a cousin and can be substituted in its ground state, but the taste will be less authentic.

1. In a medium size mixing bowl, whisk together the flour, baking powder, and salt. Set aside. With a hand held or stand mixer, cream together the butter, sugar, egg, aniseed, and extract.

2. Add the creamed mixture to the flour mixture and blend with a fork, blending until no loose flour remains.

3. Mix the ¼ cup sugar and ¼ teaspoon cinnamon in a bowl. Set your oven temp to 350°F.

4. Roll a rounded tablespoon size ball of dough and place on a baking sheet lined with parchment paper. With the bottom of a glass, measuring cup or cookie stamps, press the dough to roughly ¼ inch thick round. Fill the cookie sheet with cookies, leaving ½ inch of space between each cookie. Cover tightly with plastic wrap and chill for about 15 minutes. Dredge each cookie in the cinnamon sugar and replace, sugar side up, on the baking sheet.

5. Bake for about 10-12 minutes or until cookies have very slightly turned a blond color. Cool for 5 minutes before removing to a cooling rack.

Piñon Lacey Cookies

Prep time: 75 minutes   Cook time: 11 minutes   Makes: about 24

1 ½ cups shelled piñon (pine) nuts

3 tablespoons all-purpose flour

¼ teaspoon salt

¼ teaspoon cinnamon

¾ cup white sugar

2 tablespoons heavy cream

2 tablespoons light corn syrup

5 tablespoons unsalted butter, room temperature

1 teaspoon vanilla extract

1 cup semisweet chocolate chips

2 teaspoons chile powder, or to taste

Piñon Lacey Cookies are a spin on the "Spanish tile" cookies, or very similar "lacey" cookies often seen in specialty stores. They can be set to cool on a rolling pin for the classic "tile shape" or just follow the recipe for a delicious Mexican chocolate sandwich cookie version.

1. Pulse 1 cup of piñons in a food processor until finely chopped. Add to a mixing bowl along with the flour, salt, cinnamon, and the rest of the whole piñons. Whisk to combine.

2. Combine sugar, cream, corn syrup, and butter in a small saucepan. Cook over medium heat, stirring occasionally until the mixture comes to a rolling boil and sugar is dissolved. Boil for one minute, then remove from heat. Stir in vanilla.

3. Pour sugar mixture into the dry ingredients and mix until combined. Chill dough for about 30 minutes. While the dough is in the fridge, set your oven to heat to 350°F. Line a baking sheet with parchment paper or a silicone baking mat.

4. Scoop round balls of dough approximately a teaspoon in size (or ½ to ¾ inch in diameter) and place on baking sheet at least 2 inches apart. They need plenty of room to spread. Bake one sheet at a time until light golden brown, about 10 minutes. Let cookies cool for 2 or 3 minutes on baking sheet before removing to a cooling rack.

5. Melt chocolate chips in the microwave on half power for about 1 minute, or until smooth when stirred. Stir in the chile powder. Spread a thin layer of chocolate on the bottom of a cookie and press the bottom of another cookie over it to make a "sandwich."

Cinnamon Sugar Dessert Sopapillas

1 batch of prepared sopapilla dough (page 16)

¹/₃ cup granulated sugar

3 tablespoons ground cinnamon

1-2 cups of your favorite chocolate sauce

Vanilla ice cream

Prep time: 15 minutes   Cook time: 10 minutes   Serves: 8

Although not exactly traditional, dessert Sopapillas are often served in surrounding states and Tex-Mex restaurants. This recipe makes a fun and delicious dessert that would impress anyone, traditional or not.

1. Mix sugar and cinnamon together, and place in a medium sized bowl.

2. Fry sopapillas (page 16) according to recipe. After each is done frying, immediately place into the cinnamon sugar bowl and coat with the mixture.

3. Tear (or bite) a corner of a sopapilla and drizzle chocolate sauce inside. Serve with a scoop of ice cream.

Tres Leches Cake

1 stick unsalted butter at room temp

1 cup whole milk

4 egg whites

1 box vanilla cake mix

$\frac{1}{2}$ teaspoon cinnamon

1 (14 ounce) can sweetened condensed milk

1 (12 ounce) can evaporated milk

1 cup Horchata (page 84)

1 teaspoon vanilla

1 container whipped topping

Prep time: 3 $\frac{1}{2}$ hours   Cook time: 35 minutes   Makes: 12 servings

Tres Leches means "three milks" in Spanish and true to its name, the classic poke cake is soaked with three different milks in the recipe. If you don't have easy access to horchata, substitute half & half or heavy cream instead.

1. Preheat oven to 325°F. Grease and flour the bottom and sides of a 13X9-inch baking dish and set aside.

2. Place butter and whole milk in a saucepan and set to medium heat to completely melt the butter. When melted, remove from heat and set aside. While the butter and whole milk heat, beat egg whites to stiff peaks and set aside.

3. Whisk or sift the box of cake mix and cinnamon together. Mix in the milk and melted butter mixture and then gently fold in the whipped egg whites with a spatula.

4. Pour into your prepared pan and bake cake according to time listed on package, or until a toothpick inserted into the center comes out clean. Remove cake and cool for 10 minutes.

5. Poke holes in the cake all over with a skewer about $\frac{1}{2}$ inch apart. Whisk the sweetened condensed milk, evaporated milk, horchata, and vanilla in a 4-cup measuring cup. Drizzle all over the surface of the cake $\frac{1}{2}$ cup at a time, giving the milk mixture time to soak in. Set cake on the counter for about 15 minutes, then chill uncovered for at least three hours. Remove and frost with whipped topping. Serve.

Green Chile Apple Pie

1 box premade double-crust pie crust

2 tablespoons all-purpose flour

1 teaspoon grated lemon zest

³/₄ cup granulated sugar

1 tablespoon brown sugar

¹/₄ teaspoon ground nutmeg

¹/₄ teaspoon ground cinnamon

¹/₈ teaspoon ground allspice

¹/₄ teaspoon salt

7 ounces chopped medium to hot green chiles (about 1 cup)

4 pounds of Gala apples, peeled and sliced ¹/₄ inch thick

1 tablespoon fresh lemon juice

¹/₃ cup shredded cheddar cheese

1 egg white, beaten lightly

1-2 tablespoons turbinado sugar

Prep time: 1 hour   Cook time: 1 hour   Makes: 12 servings

The sweet heat and unique taste of this famous New Mexican apple pie is fun, delicious, and surprisingly easy to make. Grab a friend to help peel and chop apples and you'll be enjoying a slice in no time!

1. Place pie crusts unopened on the counter to come to room temperature. While waiting for the pie crusts to warm, add flour, lemon zest, sugar, brown sugar, nutmeg, cinnamon, allspice, salt, and green chiles to a large Dutch oven or 6-quart pot.

2. Peel and slice apples, placing them into the pot with the spices and stir to coat. Set the apples over medium heat and cover. Cook, stirring occasionally, for 15-20 minutes until the apples are soft. Stir in lemon juice. Scoop filling out with a slotted spoon onto a rimmed baking sheet to cool, discarding excess liquid in the pot.

3. Unwrap one pie crust on a clean work surface. Gently place it into the pie plate, pressing it down into the bottom and along the sides. Sprinkle the cheddar cheese evenly into the bottom of the crust. Cover with plastic wrap and place in the fridge to chill and set.

4. Move an oven rack to the lowest position and set oven to 500°F. When the apples have cooled, remove the pie plate from the fridge and fill it to the brim with the green chile apple filling. Unroll the second pie crust. Cut a large "X" in the center, or get decorative and cut it into lattice strips. Place the crust on top of the pie and crimp the top and bottom pie crusts together in a decorative fashion.

5. Brush egg white over the top crust with a finger or a pastry brush. Sprinkle turbinado sugar over the crust. Place pie on a baking sheet and then on the bottom rack of the oven. Change heat to 425°F and bake for 25 minutes.

6. Rotate the pie and lower the temperature to 350°F. Bake for an additional 30-35 minutes until the crust is nice and golden brown. If the crust is browning too deeply, carefully cover the edges with aluminum foil to prevent more browning. Remove from the oven and let cool for 1 hour and serve.

Index

About the Author

Growing up in New Mexico, Emily was inspired to be a great cook by all the delicious New Mexican food (and chile!) that was a part of her life. After selling a cake for $135 at a cake auction, she was inspired to share her delicious New Mexican recipes along with other country recipes and desserts on her blog, The Goldilocks Kitchen, and in her cookbooks. Emily is a scholar of multiple culinary arts as well as fine arts and continues to hone her skills today. When she's not frying perfectly puffy golden sopapillas or hot-air ballooning, she is keeping up with her faith and family in the Albuquerque metro area.

Acknowledgments

So many wonderful friends, family, and fellow bloggers have made this book possible. I want to thank my husband, Camron, my father, Kirk, and my in-laws; Melanie and Gary, for all the babysitting and recipe testing they so kindly agreed to. Shatzi Webster for inspiring me to begin my food blogging journey, DeAnn Sena O'Connor for being a fantastic Graphic Design Consultant, Genevieve Contreras for teaching me many of her grandmother's New Mexican recipes all those years ago, and my children for being so patient with me.

Inspiration for this book and its recipes came from many resources. Along with living in New Mexico for 30 years and learning about the wonderful foods and cultures from the friends who have blessed my life, my library of cookbooks also came in very handy for research purposes. Each of the recipes in this book is the result of countless hours of recipe testing in my home kitchen and is unique to me.

This book is dedicated to my mother, Pam, whom I'm sure gave a little extra help from Heaven to make this project possible.

Made in the USA
Monee, IL
28 October 2021